YOUR KNOWLEDGE HAS VALUE

Bibliographic information published by the German National Library:

The German National Library lists this publication in the National Bibliography; detailed bibliographic data are available on the Internet at http://dnb.dnb.de .

Imprint:

Copyright © 2013 GRIN Verlag
Print and binding: Books on Demand GmbH, Norderstedt Germany
ISBN: 9783346059383

This book at GRIN:

https://www.grin.com/document/506798

Maximilian Konrad

Robert Michels reconsidered. Is there an "Iron Law of Oligarchy"?

GRIN Verlag

GRIN - Your knowledge has value

Since its foundation in 1998, GRIN has specialized in publishing academic texts by students, college teachers and other academics as e-book and printed book. The website www.grin.com is an ideal platform for presenting term papers, final papers, scientific essays, dissertations and specialist books.

Visit us on the internet:

http://www.grin.com/

http://www.facebook.com/grincom

http://www.twitter.com/grin_com

Robert Michels reconsidered: Is there an 'Iron Law of Oligarchy'?

This paper critically assesses Robert Michels' famous 'Iron Law of Oligarchy'. After a summary of Robert Michels' argument, it challenges his assumption that this law of oligarchy is 'iron' by giving counter-examples for egalitarian societies in Africa. As these egalitarian societies come along with serious disadvantages, the Athenian model of democracy by lot is presented as a more viable alternative to the law of oligarchy. The conclusion applies this model of democracy by lot to Robert Michels' starting point: the political party.

Introduction

Yes, there is a law of oligarchy. But this law of oligarchy is not 'iron', it is man-made. By calling it 'iron' Robert Michels (2004: 342-356) commits the cardinal fault of the bourgeois social scientist: he reifies and naturalizes societal processes (Marx 1953: 76-90). In order to assess this law of oligarchy, why it is man-made, and how it could be made more democratic, this essay advances in three steps: first of all, the law of oligarchy and the reasons for its existence shall be outlined along the writings of Michels. But instead of taking this law as something natural, it will be shown in a second step that it is contingent on the hierarchical organization of contemporary western society. Anthropological evidence for egalitarian societies will serve as a counterexample. But while an egalitarian society may seem utterly utopian under the currently given societal organization, in a third step the Athenian model of democracy by lot shall be presented as a more viable path toward a more democratic democracy. In a concluding remark the implications a democracy by lot could have on parties and democracy as a whole will be assessed.

The Law of Oligarchy

Robert Michels' argument about the 'iron law of oligarchy' is as simple as it is powerful. It derives its power from the very organization of society itself. While democracy means rule of the people, oligarchy is the rule of the few, the rule of a powerful elite. Robert Michels now argues that democracy is actually not the rule of the people, but always the rule of interchanging elites. Instead of being a description of reality, democracy is merely a legal principle (Michels 2004: 342).

For Michels this follows from the hierarchical organization of society: "Who says organization, says oligarchy." (Michels 2004: 365) This conclusion follows from the observation that in every organization there is a "dominion of the elected over the electors, of the mandatories over the mandators, of the delegates over the delegators." (Michels 2004: 365) Apart from the hierarchical organization of society, further causes of this law of oligarchy are the need for a technically skilled elite (Michels 2004: 61-81) and the psychological needs (Michels 2004: 85-92) of the masses for leadership. Democracy thus merely means that the minority group of the ruling is not based on a hereditary principle like in an aristocracy, but that the people can from time to time decide which elite will rule them (Michels 2004: 355).

Contrary to Pareto, Michels believes that this exchange of elites will never be complete, but that there will be a constant contest for power with new elites rising, challenging the old ones and assimilating themselves to them once they have reached power (Michels 2004: 354-355). A process that can very well be studied in contemporary politics, especially with parties on the left.[1]

Although the ruling elites and the aspiring-to-be elites may also represent interests of the masses, ultimately they will mainly look on their own advantages, which sometimes coincide with the interests of the represented, but often, especially in decisive situations, will be more conservative and oriented towards the preservation of their own power position (Michels 1962: 353). Michels has been critized for not giving enough account to the interest representational aspect of democracy (Lipset 2004: 28-30), but he would probably argue that the interest to preserve their own power overrules the altruistic motivations of the elites.

Even in a Marxian account of history where at some point the state will be crushed by the proletariat and the means of production will become common property, there will still remain a need for a bureaucracy to organize the means of production (Michels 2004: 347). To repeat: "Who says organization, says oligarchy." (Michels 2004: 365) Even in this kind of state there would therefore be a ruling elite within the bureaucracy. The history of the Soviet Union has proven Michels right. But why is this law of oligarchy 'iron'? For Michels this rests on the assumption that "Leadership is a necessary phenomenon in every form of social life." (Michels 2004: 364). Challenging this assumption is the aim of the following section.

---

[1] Just think of the German Green Party supporting the War in Afghanistan and of Secretary of Foreign Affairs Joschka Fischer changing from trainers to suits.

Egalitarian Societies

Most Westerners would probably readily agree with Michels assumption about the necessity of leadership. But this assumption suddenly becomes far less tenable once one starts looking at non-western societies. The anthropologist James Woodburn does this fascinatingly in his work on egalitarian societies, his main examples being the !Kung Bushmen of Botswana and the Hadza of Tanzania (Woodburn 1982: 433). He uses the term *egalitarian* to describe societies in which equalities of power, wealth and status are not merely propagated by law, but are actually realized (Woodburn 1982: 432). Thus, even if a hierarchical society always necessitates oligarchy, society does not always necessitate hierarchy. In order to give a firmer grounding to this contention of one of Michels basic premises, and in order to evaluate the implications of this egalitarian alternative to a hierarchical society, some more details shall be outlined.

Characteristic for both the !Kung and the Hadza is that they are hunter-gatherer societies (Woodburn 1982: 432). But as there exist many non-egalitarian hunter-gatherer societies, further differentiation is necessary: Within the hunter-gatherer societies there can be made a distinction between immediate-return systems and delayed-return systems. In an immediate-return system people consume the food they hunt and gather either on the spot, or soon after. Storage of food does not exist and the tools and weapons necessary to hunt and gather are easily built (Woodburn 1982: 432).

In a delayed-return system the yields of labor are not consumed on the spot, but are distributed later in a more complex way, taking into account the labor applied in a more complex way of hunting and gathering, for example the construction of complex tools like nets, boats or beehives (Woodburn 1982: 433). Thus, all delayed-return systems necessitate a certain amount of organization in distributing the food and producing the means to obtain it. This necessary amount of organization is inimical to equality. Obviously, by storing seeds, protecting the crops etc. all agricultural systems are delayed-return systems and therefore require organization, leadership and oligarchy (Woodburn 1982: 433).

But while this accounts for the reasons delayed-return systems need organization and therefore are non-egalitarian, it does not yet fully explain how immediate-return systems maintain being egalitarian. Without going into any details, just the three main characteristics (Woodburn 1982; 2005: 22-23) of these societies preventing individuals from accumulating personal power shall be outlined.

3

First of all, every member, regardless of age, kinship or gender, has direct and immediate access to food (Woodburn 1982: 437-439; 2005: 22-23). Second of all, everybody can exercise the freedom to move around and to associate himself with a new community (Woodburn 1982: 435; 2005: 23). Thirdly, even if somebody accumulates more than necessary for himself there is a very strong ideology to share with the rest of the community (Woodburn 1982: 442-444; 2005: 23). Through the equal access to food for everybody and through the obligation to share the accumulation of wealth and the development of dependency structures is prevented. Even if dependency structures arise, they can easily be evaded by actualizing the freedom to move around (Woodburn 1982: 445; 2005: 21, 23).

Michels' assertion that "Leadership is a necessary phenomenon in every form of social life." (Michels 2004: 364) has to be departed in face of these obvious counterexamples. But it does not have to be departed completely: the above-described societies have one serious flaw, and this is their reliance on immediate-return and the ensuing non-organization of society. As our own society is heavily based on organization and on the existence of private property, any transition to a non-organizational, property-less and egalitarian society is highly improbable. Any Marxian attempts in this direction have failed. Also, the abolition of societal organization would at the same time abolish all kinds of achievements like hospitals, schools and technology, which seems highly undesirable. Leadership is thus a necessary phenomenon, as long as one does not want to abandon societal organisation. Robert Michels actually even did account for this, when he refuted the "cloudland of individualist anarchism" (Michels 2004: 350) as the impossible alternative to an organized society. The law of oligarchy is thus not iron, but man-made by our decision for an organized society.

This however provides a rather pessimistic outlook for the possibility of democracy. In the following section there shall therefore be made a suggestion for a more democratic, and less oligarchic democracy.

More democratic democracy

Michels himself (2004: 63-78) has already convincingly refuted the concept of direct democracy because of the susceptibility of the masses to demagogues. The positive potentials of deliberative democracy on party leaders (Teorell 1999) can probably be refuted on the same terms. Therefore here democracy by lot shall be put forward as a more democratic form of democracy. The Athenian democracy shall serve as inspiration and example for this proposal.

By the term 'democracy by lot' a system is described in which democratic rule is not, or at least not exclusively, carried out by a popular vote, but by a lot. In Athens this worked in a way that for most offices, all citizens interested in that office could put forward their names and then the lot would decide. To ensure the responsible conduct of the office endowed to them, at the end of their term the officeholders were held accountable by the assembly. Only relatively few offices, which needed specialist knowledge (e.g. the *strategoi*), were elected (Taylor 2007: 323-325; Bouleau 2011: 69-70).

Sociological research conducted on the outcomes of this system has shown, that in the elected offices a significantly higher proportion of officeholders was from a wealthy background and from the area near the city of Athens or the city itself. Contrary to this, the background of the officeholders determined by lot was both geographically and economically much more diverse, representing the actual sociological composition of the Athenian citizenship far closer (Taylor 2007: 329-337). Aristotle even claimed in his Politeia that "the use of the lot is regarded as democratic, and the use of the vote as oligarchic" (Aristotle Pol 1294b 7-9, quoted after Taylor 2007: 323).

The use of the lot is so democratic, because it actually enables a rule by the people, and not only by a narrow elite. Although the office holders are still only a part of the people, their selection is based on a far more objective principle than in a vote. A vote favors the rhetorically brilliant, ambitious, wealthy and powerful in each society, whereas the lot does not look at the person gaining the office. Before the lot, contrary to the vote, everybody is actually equal. This means that groups factually disfavored by contemporary democracy have equal chances to hold an office.[2]

An obvious problem arising in this model is the legitimation of rulers who were chosen by chance, and not by consent of the ruled. But first of all, every ruled person had and has a realistic chance to become a ruler if he wants to, which is certainly not the case in a democracy by vote, where there exists only a very theoretical possibility, strongly constrained by political practice. Second of all, democracy by vote maybe has an even more severe problem of legitimation because the loosing minority is not at all represented in government. Also, the ruling class in a democracy by vote is just an oligarchical elite, a 'political class' detached from 'the people' (Michels 2004: 353), whereas in a democracy by lot it is much more firmly interwoven with the people.

---

[2] In Athens however these groups were not even considered to be citizens.

5

The most obvious objection to a selection by lot is the maybe-lacking competency of the potential officeholders. On the one hand this danger could be limited by introducing minimum levels of age, work experience, education etc. for certain positions. On the other hand the same danger of lacking competency is equally existent in a democracy by vote, where above all rhetorical and Machiavellian skills make up for politicians. Also, it is implicitly assumed in a democracy, that every citizen has the abilities to decide over the future course of the state, although that may not be true in each individual case. Maybe true democracy by the people even means to have rulers as competent or incompetent as the people. This could be the price to be paid for not being ruled by a self-reproducing elite.

But in any case, it has to be stated that even in a democracy by lot, society still has an organization and the rule of oligarchy still applies, no matter if the oligarchy is determined in a more democratic way or not.

Conclusion

But how could the democracy by lot work within a party, the starting point for Michels deliberations? (Michels 2004: 5-7) The most crucial decision would be, whether everybody, who wants to, could become a party official, or if this option should only be open to party members.

The first solution would open up parties to society and tend towards a more holistic concept of the party. In this conception people would not need a very strong ideological affiliation to become a party official. This might mean that much less politically committed persons could consider it attractive to become a party official and influence the party course with their ideas. Strong ideologies would probably be blurred and the tendency would rather go towards a more deliberative model of politics focused on single issues, in which party positions would gradually whither away for individuals and their opinions (Cf. Giddens 1994).

The second solution, restricting party offices to party members, would leave the party system as such as it were, but would promote a much more democratic access to positions of power within the party. It would probably prevent the development of a detached party elite, and the new elite from the basis would probably be more ideologically and less Machiavellianly motivated. This would effect that even in decisive moments they would go for the option best for the aims of the party, and not for the preservation of their position. This might result in a more ideologized political process in general, which would put the contestative elements of politics to the front, an idea that would certainly appeal to Michels (2004: 353).

But which of these two options is best, whether a more deliberative, or a more contestative model of politics is more desirable, is yet another question to be discussed (cf. Mouffe 2005). In any case, a democracy by lot would seriously weaken the law of oligarchy.

Bibliography

Bouleau, N. (2011), Risk and Meaning: Adversaries in Art, Science and Philosophy. EBook: Springer.

Giddens, A. (1994), Beyond left and right: the future of radical politics. Cambridge: Polity Press.

Lipset, S. (2004), 'Introduction' in Michels, R. Political Parties, A sociological study of the Oligarchical Tendencies of Modern Democracy, London: Transaction Publishers, 15-42.

Marx, K. (1953) Das Kapital Kritik der politischen Ökonomie Erster Band Der Produktionsprozess des Kapitals, Berlin: Dietz Verlag.

Michels, R. (2004) Political Parties, A sociological study of the Oligarchical Tendencies of Modern Democracy, London: Transaction Publishers.

Mouffe, C. (2005) On The Political, London: Routledge.

Taylor, C. (2007) From the whole citizen body? The sociology of Election and Lot in the Athenian Democracy Hesperia: Journal of the American School of Classical Studies at Athens 76 (2): 323-345.

Teorell, J. (1999), A Deliberative Defence of Intra-Party Democracy Party Politics 5 (3): 363-382.

Woodburn, J. (1982) 'Egalitarian Societies' Man, New Series 17 (3), 431-451.

Woodburn, J. (2005) 'Egalitarian Societies Revisited' in Widlok, T., Tadesse, W. (eds.), Property and Equality Volume 1, Ritualisation, Sharing, Egalitarianism, New York: Berghahn Books, 18-31.